Can the Earth Survive?

Threats to Our Water Supply

Louise Spilsbury

rosen publishing's
rosen central

New York

Published in 2010 by The Rosen Publishing Group Inc.
29 East 21st Street, New York, NY 10010

First Edition

Commissioning editor: Jennifer Sanderson
Designer: Jane Hawkins
Picture researcher: Kathy Lockley
Illustrator: Ian Thompson
Proofreader: Susie Brooks
Consultant: Steph Warren

Library of Congress Cataloging-in-Publication Data

Spilsbury, Louise.
   Threats to our water supply / Louise Spilsbury.
      p. cm. — (Can the earth survive?)
   Includes bibliographical references and index.
   ISBN 978-1-4358-5352-2 (library binding)
   ISBN 978-1-4358-5480-2 (paperback)
   ISBN 978-1-4358-5481-9 (6-pack)
   1. Water-supply—Juvenile literature. 2. Droughts—Juvenile
literature. 3. Water—Pollution—Juvenile literature. I. Title.
TD348.S65 2010
363.6'1—dc22

                                                  2008052468

Picture Acknowledgements:
The author and publisher would like to thank the following agencies for allowing these
pictures to be reproduced: Adrian Arbib/Still Pictures: 27; John Baker/Corbis: 32–33; Abdeljalil
Bounhar/AP/PA Photos: 48; Digital Vision/Getty: COVER, 7, 23; Nigel Hicks/ WWI/Still Pictures:
34; Chris Mattison; Frank Lane Picture Agency/Corbis: 19; Gideon Mendel/Corbis: 28-29;
Dan Porges/Still Pictures: 37; Reuters/Corbis: 26; J.B. Russel/Sygma/ Corbis: 20-21; Hartmut
Schwarzbach/Still Pictures: 22; Simon Scoones/EASI-images: 4; Jon Spaull/WaterAid: 38; James
Strachan/Stone/Getty Images: 13; Keren Su/China Span/Alamy: 31; ullstein/CARO/Sorge/Still
Pictures: 41; Simon Williams/ naturepl.com: 11

Manufactured in China

Contents

Water Resources

Water is one of Earth's most precious natural resources. Although there are alternatives to some resources, such as wood and oil, water is absolutely vital for life and there are no substitutes for it. Many people believe that Earth cannot cope with the demands humans are putting on its water supplies, yet photographs of Earth taken from space show three-quarters of the surface of the planet is covered in water. If Earth is surrounded by so much water, how could a lack of water ever become a problem?

Available Water

The fact is that less than one percent of the world's water is available to use. Almost all of the water on Earth—97.5 percent—is salty seawater that cannot be used. The remaining 2.5 percent is fresh water, but most of this is trapped in ice, glaciers, and snow, in places such as Greenland and Antarctica, and is not available for people to use.

▼ When you look at vast amounts of fresh water gushing in a waterfall like this, it is hard to believe that people could ever be short of water, but many people across the world do not have the fresh water they need.

Population Problems

The amount of water available is not decreasing—there is the same total amount of fresh water in the world today as there was in the past. However, one of the major factors affecting water supplies now is the number of people on the planet to share the resource. In 2005, there were 6.1 billion people on the planet. The United Nations (UN) predicts that the world population will increase to 9.1 billion by 2050. This means more and more water will be used, and each person will have less.

Evidence

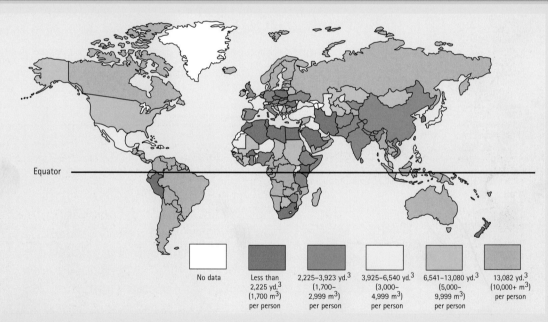

| No data | Less than 2,225 yd.^{3} (1,700 m^3) per person | 2,225–3,923 yd.^{3} (1,700– 2,999 m^3) per person | 3,925–6,540 yd.^{3} (3,000– 4,999 m^3) per person | 6,541–13,080 yd.^{3} (5,000– 9,999 m^3) per person | 13,082 yd.^{3} (10,000+ m^3) per person |

THE WORLD'S WATER

This map shows how much fresh water is available per person around the world. The lilac regions are where each person has access to lots of water. In the pink and purple regions, people are water-poor. Different factors affect the amount of water available to people in a region, but one of the most important is climate. Compare this map with the rainfall map on page 17. Some regions where people are already water-poor and where population is increasing fast, such as North Africa, also have very dry climates.

Increases in Water Use

Many people believe that even with an increase in population rates, there could still be enough water for everyone. A greater problem is that the amount of water people use has doubled in the last 30 years, and rates of use are still increasing. As well as needing water to drink, to cook with, and to wash in or clean homes, water is also used to grow the food people eat and in the manufacture of many of the products that they buy.

As standards of living increase and more people across the world buy more things, the amount of water withdrawn per person increases. For example, a person in the U.S. may use only about 13 gallons (50 liters) a day for drinking, cooking, washing, and cleaning—but when the water running from faucets is added to the amount hidden in everything people consume, from meat to cell phones, the true rate of consumption per person is about 900 gallons (3,400 liters) per day.

Evidence

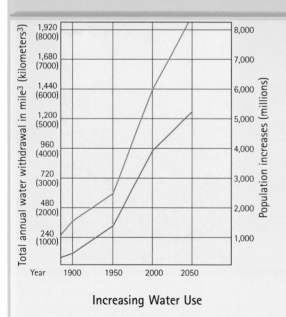

Increasing Water Use

INCREASING WATER USE

This graph shows the increase in total annual water withdrawal between 1900 and 2000, and the predicted use by 2050 as a blue line. It also shows the increase in global population for those dates as a red line. The red line is steeper than the blue line after 1950. This shows that the problem with water is not just that there are more people on the planet. The real issue is that as global standards of living improve, each person uses even more water, for example, by having showers, bathtubs, and washing machines in their homes.

Water Interdependency?

Interdependency is the way that living things depend on one another for survival. One way in which water is an interdependent resource is in international trade. When people import goods from another country, they are also effectively importing millions of gallons of water. For example, France imports cotton and other products from Egypt that have grown and been made using water from the River Nile. Countries are water interdependent because the things people buy in one place might well be draining water sources in others.

Interdependency and the Natural World

Interdependency also describes the way in which living things and the natural world depend on each other. People depend on healthy water sources. When people harm water habitats or the wildlife in them, they harm themselves, too. For example, when water is polluted, the plants and animals that live in that water are affected. If they die, the water suffers, too, because plants produce oxygen and many animals clear up waste that would otherwise build up and choke the habitat.

◀ Even people living in places surrounded by water rely on supplies of fresh water from pumps, wells, and other sources to survive.

The Lowdown on Water

Water changes form and moves between the Earth and sky constantly. It never really disappears or gets used up—the water in your faucets could have been around when dinosaurs roamed the Earth! Water travels in a large, continuous cycle called the hydrologic cycle (*hydro* means water).

▼ Each time a drop of water goes through the hydrologic cycle, it is purified. This means that animals and plants can use it again and again.

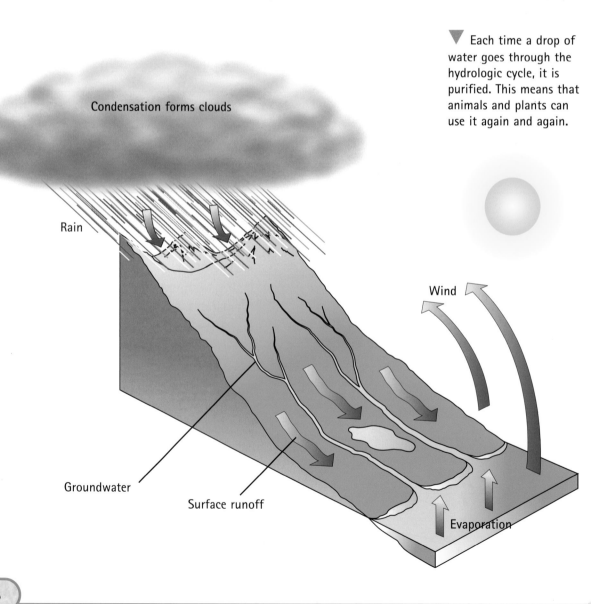

Condensation forms clouds

Rain

Groundwater

Surface runoff

Wind

Evaporation

The Hydrologic Cycle

In the hydrologic cycle, water is warmed by the Sun so it evaporates. It turns from a liquid into a gas and becomes water vapor. Water vapor is very light and floats up into the air. As it rises, the vapor begins to cool again, and it condenses and turns back into droplets of water. Billions of these tiny droplets of water form clouds. When these droplets become too heavy, they fall to the ground as rain or other kinds of precipitation, such as snow or hail. Some of this water collects on the surface of the land and is gradually warmed by the Sun, and the so the cycle continues.

Groundwater Sources

Some precipitation seeps into the ground. This process is called infiltration. The amount of water that infiltrates the soil depends on how steep the land is, the amount and type of vegetation, the type of soil and rock, and whether the soil is already saturated, or completely soaked, by water. The more cracks, holes, and openings in the ground's surface, the more infiltration occurs. This groundwater can collect in underground pools and streams, and in rocks where it may stay for a long time. Rocks saturated with water are called aquifers.

More than one-quarter of the world's population rely on groundwater supplies as their main source of useful water. People take groundwater from springs, where water bubbles to the surface through openings in the ground, or by pumping it up from below. The water table is the level below which soil and rock are saturated with water. The depth of the water table, which changes all the time, reflects the minimum level to which wells must be drilled for water extraction.

Surface Runoff

Some precipitation does not infiltrate the soil. This is called runoff. Runoff can also come from melting snow and ice. Runoff water runs off the land and collects in streams, rivers, lakes, and ponds. Some water is channeled from rivers into reservoirs. A *reservoir* is an artificial lake built to store water.

Water Habitats

▶ The Everglades depends on water from rainfall and drainage from Lake Okeechobee. This wetlands habitat has been reduced to half its original size by people's demands.

Areas of surface fresh water are not only sources of water for people, but they are also important habitats for plants and animals. Even a ditch or a puddle is filled with living things, such as water fleas and shrimps. Larger bodies of fresh water can be home to millions of species, and many of these animals and plants, such as fish and watercress, also provide food for land-based animals, including people.

Rivers

Rivers are areas of moving fresh water. They form naturally as water from rain or melted snow flows down mountains or hills. The moving water erodes paths in the earth and rocks as it flows. Rivers flow quickly down steep slopes and gradually slow as they reach flatter land. Eventually, they join the sea or flow into lakes. Many plants grow in the slower moving parts of a river and along its banks. Within rivers, there is a variety of animals, including small water snails and fish, such as pike and salmon, as well as larger animals such as otters.

Ponds and Lakes

Ponds and lakes are areas of still fresh water almost entirely surrounded by land. They form when a stream or river flows into a large dip in the land. Since the water is not moving, these bodies of fresh water rely on plants and tiny animals to keep them clean. Plants release oxygen into the water during photosynthesis, giving water animals the air they need to breathe. These animals feed on dead and waste materials to keep the water clean, ensuring the health of all water plants and animals.

Wetlands

Wetlands are areas of wet, boggy land, such as swamps, marshes, and floodplains. They are found between dry land and the deep water of coasts and rivers. A great variety of wildlife lives in freshwater wetlands—birds, amphibians, and reptiles. Wetlands also act like giant sponges. They absorb rain and flood water, and let it filter away slowly, protecting dry land behind them.

IT'S A FACT

Lake Baikal in Siberia, Russia, is the deepest lake in the world. It holds one-fifth of the world's fresh water and can be seen from space. It is home to a huge variety of animal species, including the small nerpa, one of the world's only freshwater seals.

CASE STUDY
The Everglades

The Everglades is a wetlands habitat in southern Florida. It covers 7,760 square miles (20,100 square km), which is about the size of the island of Haiti or the state of Massachusetts. The Everglades provide most of the towns and farms in southern Florida with fresh water. The area is home to rare and endangered species, such as the American crocodile, the Florida panther, and the West Indian manatee. The demand for water has meant a decrease of 50 percent in the size of the Everglades, worsening the outlook for many of its already rare animals.

People and Water

People rely on fresh water from surface and groundwater sources for a variety of reasons. The first and most important of these is for drinking water. Between 50 and 70 percent of a person's body weight is made up of water, and although humans can last for weeks without food, they can survive for only a few days without water. The human body cannot store water and an adult loses $2/3$ gallon (2.5 liters) a day through, for example, sweat and urination. It is absolutely vital that people take in fresh supplies of water every day, through drinks and through foods that contain water, such as fruit and vegetables.

Water is also vital for health and hygiene. Sanitation is the safe, clean disposal of waste products, particularly sewage and waste water from bathrooms. Using clean water to carry away bodily waste and having easy access to clean water to wash hands are vitally important factors in preventing the spread of diseases. In fact, the World Health Organisation (WHO) attributes eight out of ten illnesses in the world to unsafe water or poor sanitation. People also use water for recreation. People swim in, sail on, and play in freshwater sources such as lakes, ponds, and rivers all over the world.

Evidence

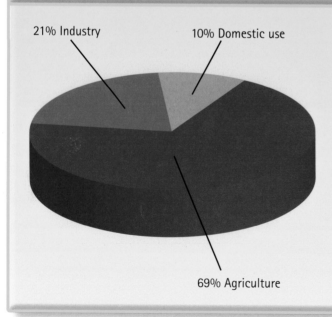

21% Industry

10% Domestic use

69% Agriculture

WATER USERS

This chart shows the proportions of water taken by agriculture, industry, and domestic users around the world. The proportions for the different activities differ dramatically for specific regions. For example, in some parts of Asia, the share of water used by farming may be as high as 86 percent, but in parts of Europe, it is as low as 38 percent. People in North America and the U.K. use the most water for industry.

Water sources, such as rivers and wetlands, directly supply people with a variety of products, such as fish to eat, poles for building materials, and reeds for making mats and baskets or for thatching houses.

Farming and Water

Agriculture uses more water than any other industry. As the world's population increases, farmers are under pressure to grow more and more food. Fields of crops that are regularly watered are much more productive than those that rely on rainfall. Although only 17 percent of the world's fields are irrigated, this land produces more than one-third of the world's food. Farmers also use water to raise farm animals, such as cattle and sheep, for the animals to drink, to grow food for them to eat, and to process their meat.

Industry and Water

Almost every product made in factories uses water during some part of the production process. Some industries, such as canned food manufacturers, also use water in their products. Others use water for washing products and machinery. Water is used to cool equipment in power stations and other factories. Hydroelectric power plants use the energy in moving water to make electricity.

Distributing Water

Water is such a vital resource that many towns, cities, and other settlements are built next to natural water supplies. The names of many settlements are even linked to water sources—Cambridge means bridge over the River Cam, for example. For settlements some distance away from freshwater sources, there are systems of pipes to bring supplies to homes and treatment plants to ensure that their water is clean. Such improved water supplies are common in more economically developed countries (MEDCs), such as the United Kingdom, Australia, and the U.S.A., whereas in less economically developed countries (LEDCs), such as some countries in Asia and Africa, water distribution systems are less common.

Water Treatment and Delivery

In countries with improved water supplies, water collected from rivers, lakes, and reservoirs is purified before being delivered to homes. It passes through several natural filters, such as gravel, and has chemicals, such as chlorine or ozone, added to it to destroy bacteria and other impurities.

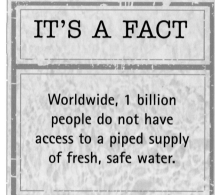

IT'S A FACT

Worldwide, 1 billion people do not have access to a piped supply of fresh, safe water.

Evidence

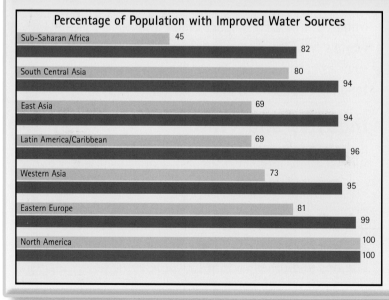

Percentage of Population with Improved Water Sources

Region	Rural	Urban
Sub-Saharan Africa	45	82
South Central Asia	80	94
East Asia	69	94
Latin America/Caribbean	69	96
Western Asia	73	95
Eastern Europe	81	99
North America	100	100

SAFE DRINKING WATER

In general, people living in rural areas (shown by light purple bars) have less access to improved water sources, or safe drinking water supplies, than city dwellers (dark purple bars). This chart also shows that less than half the people living in rural sub-Saharan Africa have access to safe water.

The water then travels through underground supply pipes to networks of smaller pipes that carry the water into homes and other buildings. Across areas of flat ground, where the water does not move by gravity alone, there may be pumping stations to move the water along the pipes.

Water Supplies in LEDCs

Many people in LEDCs do not have water piped to their homes. In Africa, less than half of the rural population has easy access to an improved water source. It is expensive and more difficult to lay pipes in remote rural areas. Often, people have to carry water from rivers, village pumps, a well, or a spring. This makes it harder to get the amount of water people need. According to the UN, everyone needs at least 13 gallons (50 liters) of water a day for drinking, washing, and cooking, but in places where people have no improved water supplies, they may be getting only a gallon or so a day.

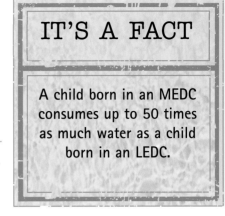

IT'S A FACT

A child born in an MEDC consumes up to 50 times as much water as a child born in an LEDC.

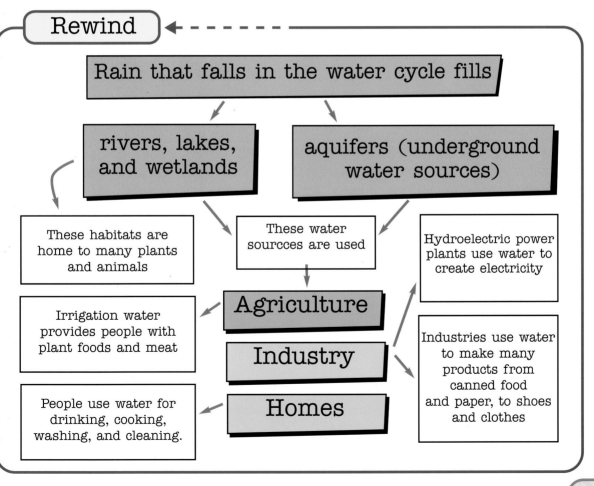

Rewind

Rain that falls in the water cycle fills

rivers, lakes, and wetlands

aquifers (underground water sources)

These habitats are home to many plants and animals

These water sourcces are used

Hydroelectric power plants use water to create electricity

Irrigation water provides people with plant foods and meat

Agriculture

Industry

Industries use water to make many products from canned food and paper, to shoes and clothes

People use water for drinking, cooking, washing, and cleaning.

Homes

What Causes Water Shortages?

There are several factors that cause water shortages. Some are out of human control, such as climate. Others are a direct result of human activity, such as the overuse or waste of water by industries, or the pollution of water.

Natural Variation

One of the major factors affecting the amount of fresh water available in a country is the climate of the region. Climate is the pattern of weather that usually occurs in a country year after year. If a place is very hot and dry, for example, people may not be able to get fresh water easily. About one-third of the world's people live in countries where there is very limited access to fresh water.

Too Little Rain

Places with hot, dry climates have very little rain. This means that there are fewer rivers and lakes. When rain does fall, some of it may evaporate rapidly in the heat and turn into water vapor before it has a chance to soak into the ground. This means that water does not filter down into the ground to create aquifers.

Too Much Rain at Once

Other parts of the world get a lot of rain, but it falls in such a short space of time that its usefulness is reduced. In Southeast Asia, there are wet and dry seasons. The wet season is known as the monsoon. During the monsoon season, which usually lasts from July to October, it can rain every day. Rain falls in such quick, heavy bursts that instead of soaking into the ground, where the rain could replenish or create groundwater sources, the water runs off the land. Monsoon rains can cause floods, where fresh water becomes polluted with mud and waste.

IT'S A FACT

Two-thirds of the global population live in areas receiving only one-quarter of the world's rainfall.

The Population Factor

An important factor linked to natural variations in climate is population. In places where the population is high, there are inevitably more people to share any available water. Australia is considered a dry country, but individual people there usually have more water than people living in Asia, which is a continent with a wetter climate. This is because there are more people in Asia to share the available water, but many parts of Australia have a low population density, or are sparsely populated. In other words, Australia has fewer people to share its water, and Asia's water sources have to be shared among many.

Evidence

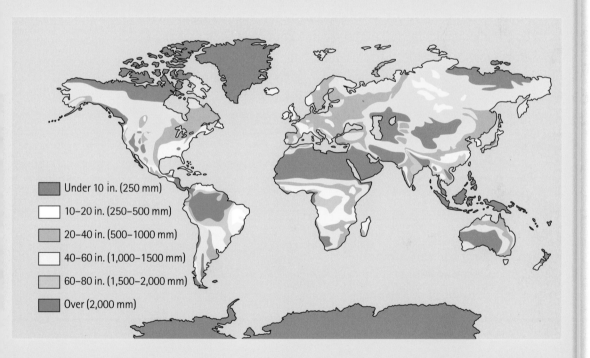

Under 10 in. (250 mm)
10–20 in. (250–500 mm)
20–40 in. (500–1000 mm)
40–60 in. (1,000–1500 mm)
60–80 in. (1,500–2,000 mm)
Over (2,000 mm)

RAINFALL PATTERNS

The map above shows the average patterns of rainfall across the world. The areas that receive the most rain are colored dark green. These are also the areas where plants grow more easily, so they look greener in real life, too. The driest regions are colored brown. In these areas, the lack of rainfall makes it harder to grow crops, so in many of these regions, the land often looks brown.

Overusing Water

As well as climate and geography, a major factor that affects the water availability in different areas is the way in which water is used. The issue is not simply that the amount of water people use is increasing because of rising populations and improvements in standards of living. In many cases, the situation is made even worse by the fact that more water is being used than necessary, and vast amounts of water are being wasted. The world's most precious resource is literally being poured down the drain.

Agriculture Overuse

Irrigation is vital for growing food, but many people believe that the agricultural industry is using unnecessarily high amounts of water. Part of the problem is that countries grow crops that are unsuited to their climates, because these are what consumers in wealthy countries want to buy. For example, in hot, water-scarce countries such as Kenya, farmers grow crops such as lettuce, arugula, baby leaf salad, snow peas, and broccoli to sell abroad. To produce just one small 1.75-ounce (50-gram) bag of salad uses up almost 13 gallons (50 liters) of water—without including the water used in washing, processing, and packaging.

▶ In this irrigation system in the U.S.A., water is piped to wheeled overhead sprayers that distribute thousands of gallons of water as they move across giant fields.

Evidence

MEAT MATTERS

This chart shows the minimum amount of water needed to produce 2.2 pounds (1 kilogram) of different types of food. It takes almost nine times the amount of water to produce 2.2 lb. (1 kg) of beef as it does to grow 2.2 lb. (1 kg) of soybeans, another protein. The high demand for meat has also led to farmers in water-scarce places raising livestock to sell for export, putting an even greater strain on water supplies.

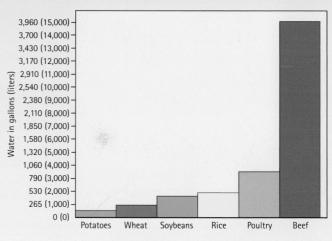

Minimun Water Needed for Food

IT'S A FACT

Up to 22 glasses of water are used in factories to create just one glass of Brazilian orange juice in a carton for the breakfast table.

Wasting Water

Another problem with agricultural use of water is waste. It is estimated that, on average, 60 percent of the water used for irrigation is wasted. Sometimes this is because too much water is sprayed on crops, so some of it soaks deep into the ground out of reach of the plants' root systems, leading some farmers to simply spray more and more water. Large amounts of water are also lost through evaporation. During the day, water sitting on the surface warms up and turns into water vapor in the air. Some farmers solve this problem by watering their crops at night, when the air is cooler and evaporation rates are greatly reduced.

CASE STUDY
Irrigation in Spain

Different plants are suited to particular climates—for example, tomatoes are 95 percent water and tomato plants need a lot of water to grow. In spite of being a particularly dry region, the province of Almería in southern Spain has become one of Europe's largest suppliers of tomatoes. Vast areas of land in Almería are covered in plastic greenhouses, inside which large amounts of tomatoes are grown to supply supermarkets almost all year round.

Tomatoes are grown in Almería by hydroponics. The plants have no direct contact with natural soil, sunlight, or rainwater. Instead, they grow in heated plastic tunnels in bags filled with grains of stone. A computer controls the amounts of fertilizers, pesticides, and water they are fed to make them grow. The advantages of this are that this once-poor region has become prosperous and people across Europe have access to reasonably priced tomatoes almost all year round.

The downside, apart from the issue of whether or not the amount of chemical fertilizers and pesticides used to raise these tomatoes is healthy or not, is that hydroponic agriculture uses more water than the environment can provide. This area of Spain is often struck by drought. The aquifers are drying up, and the soil is slowly but surely drying out and turning to dust.

The roofs of thousands of plastic greenhouses in Almería cover an area so large it can be seen from space.

Industrial Water Use

Industries use large amounts of water, but are some using more than they need? In the paper industry, for example, wood pulp is soaked in water to break it down into the fibers that are dried out and flattened to make paper. Making paper from new wood pulp uses around 8,450 gallons (32,000 liters) more water than making paper from recycled paper, which saves trees, too. Industrial use of water is set to increase because more countries are building factories where they did not exist before, and by 2025, industries could be using over one-third more water than they did in 2000. People are also buying more than they need. The production of a single microchip may use more than 85 gallons (32 liters) of water, so when people update and throw away a perfectly good computer, they are wasting water, too.

Flushed Away!

Many people believe that households in MEDCs also use much more water than they need. People in Canada, for example, use the most water in the world, and over half of their treated water is used to keep lawns green. The amount of water used could be reduced if water-efficient appliances were installed in homes. A typical family of four in the United States uses about 53 gallons (200 liters) of water every day. One-third of the family's household water is used just to flush the toilet. Toilets equipped with a water-saving device save a quart of water on each flush. Leaking pipes also waste a lot of water, and because often it costs more to repair a leaking pipe than it does to put more water into the supply, leaks are often left unrepaired.

Pollution

Around the world, up to 2 million tons of waste and chemicals pour into water sources each and every day. Water pollution damages rivers, lakes, and other water supplies all over the world. It is becoming increasingly expensive and difficult to purify water, and some kinds of pollution are impossible to remove. Pollution drastically reduces the amount of clean water available for people to use.

Sewage and Cities

Although wastewater treatment plants are now more common in MEDCs, nine out of ten cities in LEDCs release untreated sewage into rivers, lakes, and other water sources every day. Sewage waste contains bacteria that pollute freshwater sources. Cities with efficient drainage systems still have pollution problems as more and more toxic chemicals and bleaches in cleaning and bathroom products are poured into drains.

▼ In many parts of the world, where water is not piped to villages or homes, people may have no choice but to wash in and use water from water sources that are polluted.

▶ Many industrial plants around the world use fresh water to carry waste away from their factories into nearby water supplies, such as rivers and streams.

City Pollutants

Pollutants can also come from parking lots, yards, gardens, driveways, sidewalks, and streets. Rainwater or melted snow can wash pollutants, such as oil that has leaked from cars, litter, and garden fertilizers, into gutters. In some areas, the drains carry this polluted water to a water treatment facility, but in others, it is transported to a nearby river, lake, stream, or wetland.

Chemical and Industrial Waste

Some chemical and industrial waste flows directly into waterways. For example, the Ganges is the longest river in India, and many of the factories along its length dump chemical waste directly into the water. In some places, factories bury waste underground and these pollutants gradually drain into groundwater sources. Industrial accidents or disasters, although rare, can also cause pollution. For example, in 1996, massive amounts of chemical waste leaked from a copper mine in the Philippines into a river, contaminating the fresh water so badly that the river was virtually destroyed.

Some pollutants reach water sources as runoff. Fertilizers and pesticides are chemicals that farmers use to help crops to grow and to get rid of insect pests that damage crops. Rain washes some of these chemicals off fields and into streams and rivers, or they seep through the soil into groundwater sources, polluting previously safe drinking water.

IT'S A FACT

In the U.S.A., farm animals produce 130 times more slurry (sewage waste) than people. Overall, farming is responsible for 70 percent of the water pollution in the entire country.

Changing Land Use

To increase the area of land that can be built on or the amount of food that can be grown, often, water sources are drained and waterways are diverted. The positive results of this are more land for people to live on, more electric power, and better crops. However, changing land use has also caused a dramatic reduction in water supplies.

Diversions and Dams

Many rivers are diverted from their natural course to take water for irrigation. Often, channels are built to carry some of the water from a river elsewhere. Dams are also built to collect water in reservoirs for irrigation, to pump to homes, or to use in hydroelectric power plants. Irrigation provides food for billions of people, and hydroelectric power stations are a vital form of electricity production for many. However, when water is diverted in this way, less water undoubtedly reaches people who live farther downstream.

Draining Wetlands

Around the world, many wetlands have been drained. The water has been pumped out of them so that homes, farms, and factories can be built on the newly dry land. For example, in the Netherlands, two-fifths of the country's land has been reclaimed from water and people now live, work, and farm on areas that were once wetlands. In some places, wetlands have been dug out or dredged to open shipping canals to the sea. When salt water from the sea flows into these rivers, the water within them is no longer fresh and drinkable.

Concrete and Cities

The rapid growth of cities has had an impact on groundwater sources. When soil is covered over by concrete streets and sidewalks, rainwater no longer drains through the earth and filters into groundwater sources deep below the surface. Instead, the rain runs off the paved areas into sewers, rivers, or straight into the sea. This means that aquifers are no longer being slowly refilled and freshwater supplies are being depleted.

CASE STUDY
Murder of Marshlands

Up until the 1970s in southern Iraq, there was a vast wetland area so full of wildlife that it was known as the Garden of Eden. Since then, 30 dams have been built. These broke up the rivers that flowed into the region, reducing the amount of water feeding the marshes. Added to the dams, in the 1990s, a massive drainage scheme was started. Today, the marshlands of southern Iraq have been almost completely destroyed and left as desert.

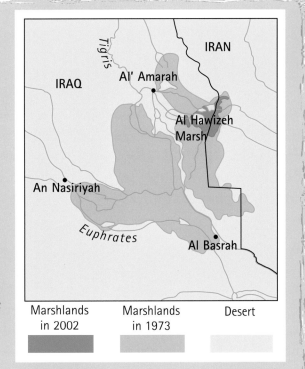

Marshlands in 2002　　Marshlands in 1973　　Desert

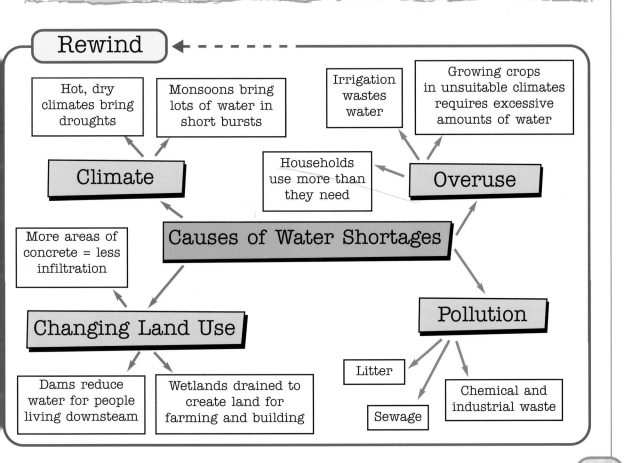

Rewind

Hot, dry climates bring droughts

Monsoons bring lots of water in short bursts

Irrigation wastes water

Growing crops in unsuitable climates requires excessive amounts of water

Climate

Households use more than they need

Overuse

More areas of concrete = less infiltration

Causes of Water Shortages

Changing Land Use

Pollution

Dams reduce water for people living downsteam

Wetlands drained to create land for farming and building

Litter

Sewage

Chemical and industrial waste

The Impact of Water Shortages

When an airplane crashes and people die, it makes front-page news. But every day, enough people to fill ten jumbo jets die from diseases linked to dirty water.

A Lack of Hygiene

About two-fifths of the world's people do not have water for sanitation—to wash, clean, and dispose of sewage and waste water safely. When hygienic conditions are not maintained, diseases spread quickly. Water polluted with human or animal feces becomes a breeding ground for bacteria that cause serious diseases. People become infected with a disease when they collect, bathe in, or drink the water. For example, more than two million people die from diarrhea every year. In places where clean water supplies have been provided, so that people can use soap and water to wash their hands, the incidence of this killer condition has dropped by 40 percent.

IT'S A FACT

Every eight seconds, a child dies of a waterborne disease and around the world, nearly two million people die each year from diseases caused by unsafe water.

Standing Water

When water is scarce, people often collect rainfall in containers. This has detrimental consequences because insects, such as mosquitoes, lay their eggs in areas of uncovered still water. These insects spread diseases, such as malaria and dengue, when they bite humans. Over a million people a year die from malaria and another 20,000 people die after being infected with dengue.

▶ When people have no choice but to use dirty water, there are outbreaks of life-threatening diseases such as cholera and typhoid.

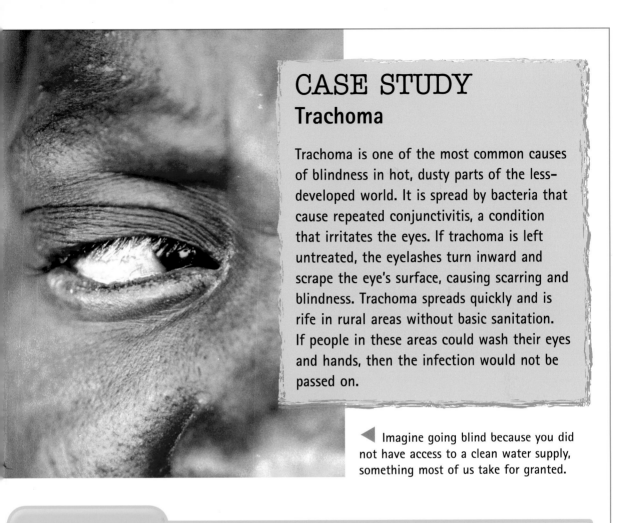

CASE STUDY
Trachoma

Trachoma is one of the most common causes of blindness in hot, dusty parts of the less-developed world. It is spread by bacteria that cause repeated conjunctivitis, a condition that irritates the eyes. If trachoma is left untreated, the eyelashes turn inward and scrape the eye's surface, causing scarring and blindness. Trachoma spreads quickly and is rife in rural areas without basic sanitation. If people in these areas could wash their eyes and hands, then the infection would not be passed on.

◀ Imagine going blind because you did not have access to a clean water supply, something most of us take for granted.

Evidence

DIRTY WATER DEATHS

Over 80 percent of the diseases that affect people in LEDCs, including cholera and typhoid, are related to water shortages or dirty water. This pie chart shows the number of deaths linked to dirty water in 2000. Over two-thirds of the deaths occured in Africa and Southeast Asia, places with the largest populations and the lowest number of improved water supplies.

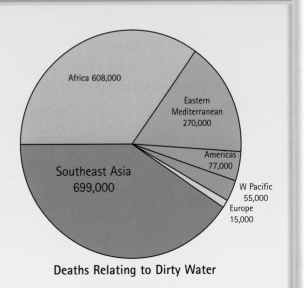

Africa 608,000

Eastern Mediterranean 270,000

Americas 77,000

W Pacific 55,000

Europe 15,000

Southeast Asia 699,000

Deaths Relating to Dirty Water

Hunger and Poverty

The lack of fresh, clean water is a major reason why many people around the world are living in a state of hunger and poverty. A lack of water affects employment opportunities and the amount of money people can earn. It also means it is harder to grow enough food for a country's population. When water shortages affect food production, countries often have to import food, which is more expensive than growing their own and often makes matters worse.

▲ Many children in Swaziland spend four to six hours each day fetching water. These children have to walk to collect water before they go to school in the mornings and in the evenings before it gets dark.

Drought

In places with hot, dry climates, such as Somalia in Africa, droughts can last for years. When this happens, it is almost impossible for people to grow crops. Without crops they, and any animals they were keeping for food, go hungry. As well as growing food to eat themselves, many people in LEDCs rely on farming for an income, so when they cannot grow crops, they do not have anything to sell to get money to buy food or water from someone else.

Loss of Earnings

Water shortages also keep people in poverty, because waterborne diseases prevent them from working. Many people who contract diseases from infected water supplies, or because of a lack of sanitation, are forced to stay at home while they recover, if they are lucky enough to survive. For example, in the tropical regions of Africa, each bout of malaria can cost a person ten working days and therefore ten days' pay. When you add that sum of money to the cost of treatment, if they have to pay for that, too, there is a vast amount of money lost.

Missed Education

Water shortages rob many children of their chance of an education. Children may have to get up early to collect water before they go to school. This means that they arrive late to school or they are too tired to concentrate when they get there. In some countries, because schools do not have toilets, girls do not attend classes because of the lack of privacy. A lack of education has a domino effect for children when they grow up, since it makes it harder for them to get well-paid work.

Evidence

BUYING WATER

In places where there is a severe shortage of water many people buy water from vendors who sell water from mobile tanks. This bar chart shows the difference in price in US dollars that poor people have to pay for their water compared to what wealthier people in the same country, who have fresh, clean water piped directly into their homes, pay.

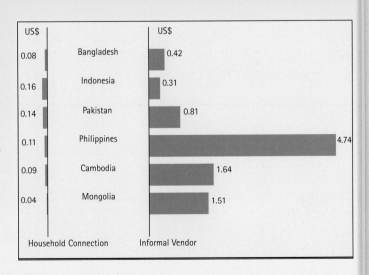

US$		US$	
0.08	Bangladesh	0.42	
0.16	Indonesia	0.31	
0.14	Pakistan	0.81	
0.11	Philippines		4.74
0.09	Cambodia	1.64	
0.04	Mongolia	1.51	
Household Connection		Informal Vendor	

Dams and Displacement

In many parts of the world, dams have been built to supply water to regions where water is in short supply or to create hydroelectric power. There is no doubt that dams benefit many people. They provide almost two-fifths of the irrigation water required worldwide, and hydroelectric power plants provide one-fifth of the world's electricity. However, dams can also have a negative impact on people's lives.

People often live alongside rivers. When new dams are built, large areas of land around rivers are cleared so that they can be flooded with water behind the dam. People who live in these regions are encouraged, or sometimes forced, to move away from the dam. So far, more than 80 million people worldwide have lost their homes because of dams.

▼ The Three Gorges dam is the biggest hydroelectric project in the world, but it has caused a great deal of controversy over the people it has displaced.

CASE STUDY
The Three Gorges Dam, China

The Three Gorges dam in China is being built to supply the world's biggest hydroelectric power plant. It will provide hydropower and water for China's growing population. Supporters say that it will also control the waters of the River Yangtse and prevent the floods that have killed thousands of people in the past. But, in order to build it, two million people have been displaced and 1,200 towns and villages will be buried under water.

Dams and Conflicts

More than 200 of the world's rivers flow through two or more different countries. The water of the River Danube, for example, is shared by a total of 17 different countries. Many countries come to agreements over how many dams can be built along their rivers or how the water should be shared between countries. However, there are often disagreements between governments. For example, water is a major issue in the ongoing conflict between Israel and Palestine in the Middle East. Much of the region's water comes from the West Bank's mountain aquifer. Israel and Israeli settlements take about 80 percent of the aquifer's flow, leaving the Palestinians with only 20 percent.

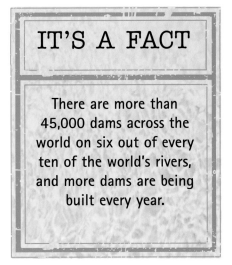

IT'S A FACT

There are more than 45,000 dams across the world on six out of every ten of the world's rivers, and more dams are being built every year.

Evidence

IMPORTING WATER

This chart shows the percentage of water different countries consume that comes from outside their borders. For example, the snow and rainfall that fill the River Ganges occur mainly in Nepal and India before the river flows into Bangladesh. About 90 percent of Bangladesh's water comes from outside the country's borders. At the other end of the scale, the United Kingdom is an island so it controls all its own water supply.

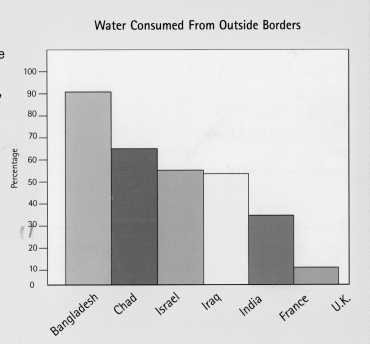

Water Consumed From Outside Borders

Groundwater Problems

Groundwater sources, or aquifers, take hundreds of years to fill up. In many parts of the world, groundwater is being removed much faster than it naturally replenishes. This causes water tables to become deeper and forces people to dig wells farther down to get the water they need. For example, in Texas, the withdrawal of irrigation water caused the Ogallala aquifer to drop so much that wells now have to be dug 100 feet (30 meters) deeper. Overextraction of groundwater means that some sources are drying up altogether, but there are also other, more surprising effects.

Sinking Cities

About half of the world's population lives in cities. To provide water and sanitation to cities, many governments pump water from nearby aquifers. Sometimes when water is removed, the underground soil compacts and the level of land at the surface drops. This is called subsidence. Subsidence can cause cracks in the land and sometimes, the cracks are so large that roads, railroad lines, buildings, and bridges as well as underground sewage or drainage pipes are damaged. Subsidence can also cause buildings in cities to sink into the ground.

Increased Salinity

Salinity is the amount of salt found in water. In some places, groundwater sources are being contaminated by salts. In some regions near the coast, for example, so much water has been pumped from underground aquifers that salty seawater has begun to soak into and pollute the freshwater sources.

Salinity can be caused when water tables rise. When farmland is overirrigated, the water can soak into the land and raise the level of the water table. Rising groundwater may bring with it dissolved salts that were stored in the ground. At the surface, the water will evaporate and leave a layer of salt. The salts kill plants and dry out the soil until it becomes infertile, making it useless for growing crops.

IT'S A FACT

Salinity has damaged almost one-quarter of all irrigated land in China and Pakistan.

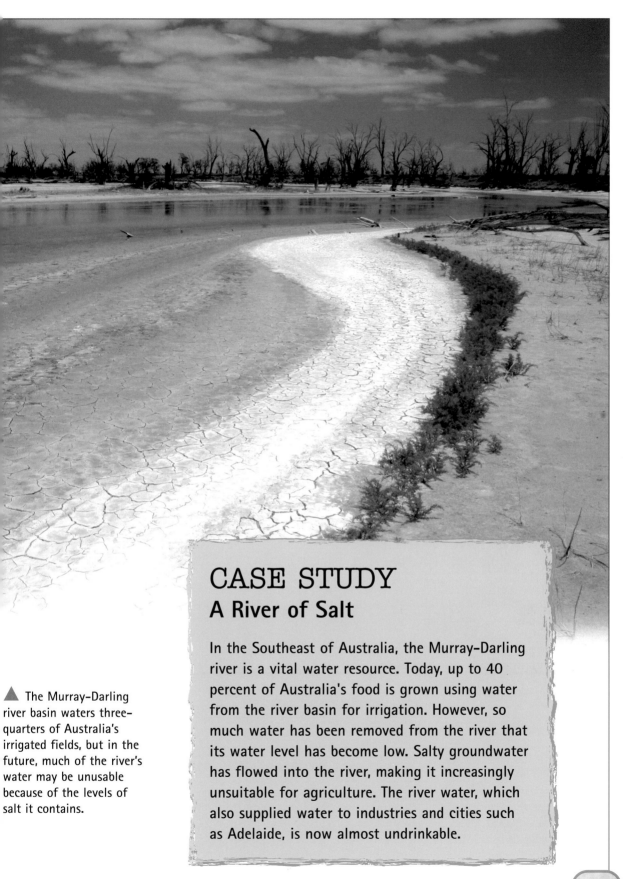

▲ The Murray–Darling river basin waters three-quarters of Australia's irrigated fields, but in the future, much of the river's water may be unusable because of the levels of salt it contains.

CASE STUDY
A River of Salt

In the Southeast of Australia, the Murray–Darling river is a vital water resource. Today, up to 40 percent of Australia's food is grown using water from the river basin for irrigation. However, so much water has been removed from the river that its water level has become low. Salty groundwater has flowed into the river, making it increasingly unsuitable for agriculture. The river water, which also supplied water to industries and cities such as Adelaide, is now almost undrinkable.

Habitats and Wildlife

Loss of water and the pollution of water sources have a huge impact on habitats and the plants and animals that live in them. The plants, animals, and the habitat are interdependent, and so rely on each other to survive. When one part of such an ecosystem is damaged, other parts are affected, too. For example, when water pollution kills plants, the fish that eat the plants may starve, as may the larger animals, such as alligators, which eat fish.

CASE STUDY
The Ganges River Dolphin

The Ganges dolphin is one of only four freshwater species of dolphin in the world. The greatest threats to the survival of this rare dolphin are the loss of its floodplain habitats and pollution caused by industrial and agricultural waste and sewage. The polluted water contaminates the fish that live in the Ganges, and these fish are then eaten by the dolphins. As a result, residues of pesticides and herbicides have been found in the bodies of dead dolphins. The presence of dolphins in a river system signals a healthy ecosystem—when dolphins start dying, it is a warning that pollution is ruining a river.

When Waters Dry Up

When too much water is taken from water sources, such as wetlands or rivers, wildlife inevitably suffers. When wetlands are drained, the many species of animals that live there lose their homes. Migrating birds travel huge distances and use wetlands like highway service stations to rest, feed, and drink. Without wetlands, many of them weaken and die before reaching their destination.

▶ The Ganges river dolphin is classed as an endangered species because there are only around 4,000 of these rare animals left.

In India, the overextraction of water from the Indus river for irrigation threatens the survival of the unique Indus river dolphin and has drastically reduced freshwater fish populations. This has an impact on other animals up the food chain, too, including humans, because fish are an important source of protein for millions of people.

Problems with Pollution

Eutrophication is an example of the damage water that pollution can do to water wildlife. Some of the pollutants that soak into waterways, such as the fertilizers intended to help land plants grow, contain nutrients. In a small pond or lake, algae feed on these nutrients and quickly grow and spread until they cover the water's surface. When the algae die, microscopic living things called microbes feed on them. The microbes multiply and start to use up the oxygen in the water. When oxygen levels in the water fall, aquatic animals cannot breathe and so they die.

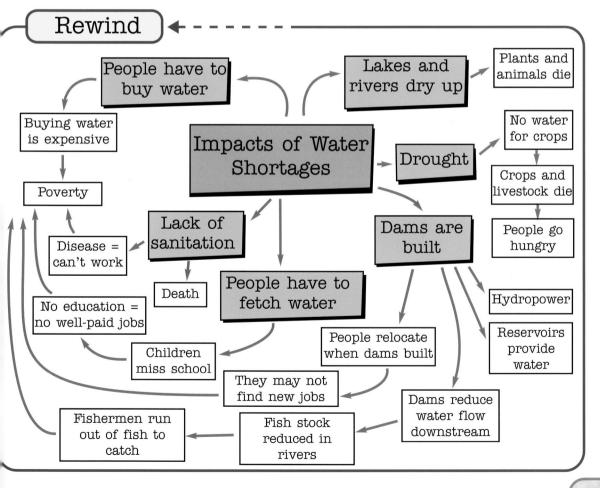

Rewind

| People have to buy water | Lakes and rivers dry up | Plants and animals die |

Buying water is expensive

Impacts of Water Shortages

Drought

No water for crops

Poverty

Crops and livestock die

Disease = can't work

Lack of sanitation

Dams are built

People go hungry

No education = no well-paid jobs

Death

People have to fetch water

Hydropower

People relocate when dams built

Reservoirs provide water

Children miss school

They may not find new jobs

Fishermen run out of fish to catch

Fish stock reduced in rivers

Dams reduce water flow downstream

Sustainable Water Use

As the world's population continues to rise, more food crops and meat are needed to feed people. The demand for water from farms, as well as factories and households, will increase. However, the natural world also needs its share of global water supplies.

Reducing Water Use

One of the ways to ensure that we all get the water we need is to conserve the water supplies we have by using water more sustainably. This means using less and recycling more.

The easiest way to save water is to use less of it. This can be done by repairing leaks, turning off dripping faucets, and with small changes to people's behavior. For example, using a low-flush toilet saves 2.6 gallons (10 liters) of water per flush.

IT'S A FACT

If people turn off the faucet while they brush their teeth, they can save about 1.5 gallons (6 liters) of water each time.

Evidence

INDUSTRIAL SAVINGS

Industries in MEDCs are finding ways of saving water, too. Some steel production plants now use less than one-quarter of the water they once used. This graph shows how industrial water use per person in the United States was cut by half between 1950 and 1990, even though the amount of goods the industries produced increased four times.

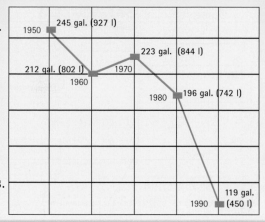

1950 — 245 gal. (927 l)
1960 — 212 gal. (802 l)
1970 — 223 gal. (844 l)
1980 — 196 gal. (742 l)
1990 — 119 gal. (450 l)

Collecting and Recycling Water

In some places, pressure on water resources is being reduced by people harvesting rainwater. Using pipes, a filter, and underground storage tanks, people collect rain that falls on roofs or driveways. Harvested rainwater is no good for drinking, but it can be used to flush toilets, water yards, and fill washing machines. In some countries, sewage water is being recycled and purified so that it can be used to water crops and grow food. In Kolkata, India, sewage is piped into lagoons. The lagoons act as natural water treatment systems, soaking up and cleaning the sewage. They also produce 6,000 tons of fish for people to eat every year.

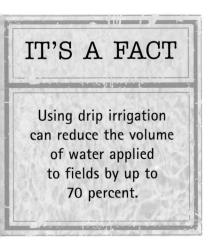

IT'S A FACT

Using drip irrigation can reduce the volume of water applied to fields by up to 70 percent.

▼ The drip irrigation water pipes running along these rows of cabbages feed water directly to the plant roots.

Farming and Fresh Water

One way that farmers are saving water is by using different methods of irrigation. In drip irrigation, water is carried across fields by pipes and hoses, and dripped through holes or nozzles that direct the water at the plant roots. This saves water because water does not gather on the soil surface and evaporate. Another vital way of saving water is for farmers to grow crops that are more suited to local climates. Consumers can also make a big difference by choosing less water-hungry crops. For example, it would help if people in the United Kingdom bought Desiree potatoes, which can be grown without irrigation there, instead of Maris Piper potatoes, which use vast amounts of water.

CASE STUDY
Do it Yourself

Sometimes small, local schemes prove to be the best way of solving water shortages in LEDCs. In a village in Mozambique, people were happy when a company built them eight new wells. The company dug the wells in marshy areas on the outskirts of the village, mainly because the soft ground was easier to dig and it meant that they made more profit. They installed hand pumps, but these were tricky to repair when broken. As a result, the project failed. The charity WaterAid then stepped in and helped the villagers to build new wells where they wanted them, closer to the village and with a winch and bucket to pull up water instead of hand pumps.

Water Management

Water management is the way in which governments or companies provide people with fresh water and make sure that water is clean and safe to use. Good water management can make a real difference to water supplies. For example, it provides more people with access to water, and reduces pollution and waste.

Good water management works in different ways. For example, in some places, water authorities check pollution levels in water sources and can fine companies if they cause pollution. Water management can also mean maintaining and improving sewage and pipe networks to prevent leakage, or putting in place temporary changes when there is a drought. In an MEDC, this may mean rationing water by enforcing watering restrictions, so that water is available for more important needs. Some MEDCs have compulsory water meters. Households must pay for the exact amount of water they use, and many people believe this reduces the amount of water people use because they want to save money.

Privatizing Water

In many LEDCs, people do not have improved water supplies. To get clean water and sanitation to more people costs a lot of money. Many governments rely on private companies to install water pipes, sewage systems, and water treatment plants. In return, the companies have the right to sell water to people for a profit. This solution has brought freshwater supplies to more people.

However, there is a downside to privatizing water. Some of the world's poorest people now pay up to 95 percent more for their water than they did before. Critics of privatization say it is better when governments control water supplies since they can balance needs, for example, by charging industries more so individuals pay less. They also say that water should be treated as a human right, not as a commodity that can be bought and sold for profit.

◀ A simple well, if it is in the right place and is easy to maintain and repair, can bring health to communities such as this one in Mozambique.

New Technologies

Many governments are looking for ways to increase their country's water supplies, and scientists and engineers are working on technologies to help meet demand. Some solutions are improvements on existing systems, such as making water systems more efficient and less prone to leaks and waste. In countries where water shortage is already at crisis point, the methods are more dramatic.

Importing Water

One way of getting water is to collect it from a wetter place and transport it to where it is needed. In Greece, giant plastic bags are filled with water from the mainland and dragged across the sea to water-short islands. The problems with this solution are that water is incredibly expensive to transport, and there is always a risk that it may become contaminated while it is in transit.

Making Fresh Water from Seawater

Desalination plants make fresh water from seawater by removing the salt. This can be done in several ways, for example, by forcing seawater through electrically charged filters that remove the salt. The problem with desalination is that, until now, most of the processes used to remove the salt from seawater used large amounts of electricity, which is both expensive and pollutes the atmosphere. Desalination also leaves large amounts of brine, which is hard to dispose of.

▶ Many countries are considering building large-scale desalination plants like this one in the United Arab Emirates. However, critics of such schemes argue that a better solution is to reduce water use.

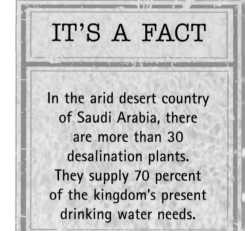

IT'S A FACT

In the arid desert country of Saudi Arabia, there are more than 30 desalination plants. They supply 70 percent of the kingdom's present drinking water needs.

Cloud Seeding and Fog Nets

Cloud seeding is when rockets, airplanes, or cannons are used to shoot dry ice into clouds. The dry ice causes the droplets of water vapor that form clouds to join together. The water droplets form snow and as they fall, they melt into rain, giving the land much-needed water. A *fog* is a mass of water droplets that gathers just above the ground. Fog nets are large rectangular nets held up like a fence by posts. When water is trapped in the net, the droplets join to form larger drops that fall into a gutter and are piped to a storage tank to be used as fresh water.

Rewind

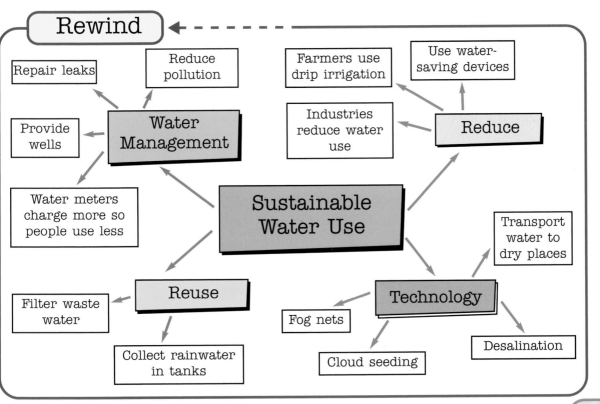

Repair leaks

Reduce pollution

Provide wells

Water Management

Water meters charge more so people use less

Farmers use drip irrigation

Use water-saving devices

Industries reduce water use

Reduce

Sustainable Water Use

Transport water to dry places

Filter waste water

Reuse

Collect rainwater in tanks

Technology

Fog nets

Cloud seeding

Desalination

Making Sure the Earth Survives

If people continue using water at the same rate as they are now, it is very likely that by 2025 the world will be facing a serious water crisis. This possible future is bleak and the situation could be made even worse by the effects of global warming.

What Effect Will Global Warming Have?

Many scientists believe that world temperatures are rising more rapidly than ever before. One impact of global warming is that ice caps and glaciers are melting. This will cause sea levels to rise, and this could mean that seawater will infiltrate and contaminate freshwater sources. Many regions rely on water that slowly melts into their rivers from mountain glaciers. Glaciers in the Himalayan mountains are predicted to shrink by one-fifth within the next 35 years. Melting ice from these glaciers feeds into the Indus and Ganges rivers, so this would be disastrous for the 500 million people who rely on these rivers for fresh water. If temperatures rise, hot, dry places are likely to receive even less rainfall, increasing the risk of droughts.

A Possible Future

If there is a severe increase in water shortages in the future, there will be less water for irrigation and this will lead to life-threatening food shortages. Millions of people could go hungry and starve to death. With water in short supply, the lack of sanitation would result in even larger numbers of people suffering from water-related diseases. As less water flows through the world's rivers, because more water is being used by growing populations, there are likely to be conflicts and wars as people fight over the way water is shared. With more and more water being taken from lakes, rivers, and ponds, more of the species of plants and animals that live in these water habitats may be lost for ever.

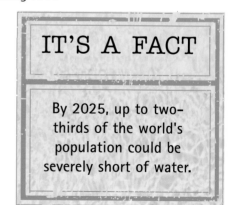

IT'S A FACT

By 2025, up to two-thirds of the world's population could be severely short of water.

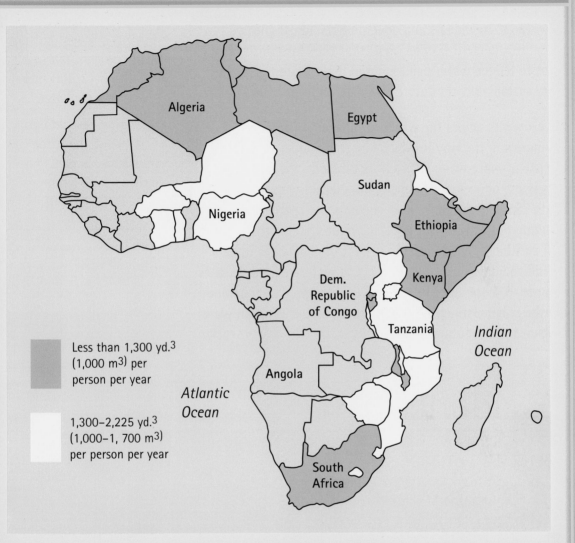

Less than 1,300 yd.^{3} (1,000 m^3) per person per year

1,300–2,225 yd.^{3} (1,000–1,700 m^3) per person per year

Algeria

Egypt

Sudan

Ethiopia

Nigeria

Dem. Republic of Congo

Kenya

Tanzania

Indian Ocean

Angola

Atlantic Ocean

South Africa

WATER IN AFRICA

This map shows that at current rates of water use, and taking into account population growth there, large parts of Africa may be suffering severe water shortages for all or part of the year. People in these areas will struggle to get the water they need to drink, cook, and clean with. As the land dries up, few, if any, crops will grow. For people in these regions, and for many others around the world, the future of water will be a matter of life and death.

The Preferable Future

There is no doubt that the amount of water the world's growing population uses will increase in the future. However, if individuals and governments across the planet recognize the water crisis that they face and take steps to reduce water pollution and make water use more sustainable, the future could be brighter.

Governments across the world can make a difference by improving the way in which water is managed. With the use of more water-efficient equipment, the amount of waste produced, for example, from leaking pipes, can be drastically reduced. And by encouraging small communities in LEDCs to develop water systems that best suit their needs, water and sanitation services to poor people could be greatly improved and water-related diseases reduced. If more cities introduce waste water recycling and rainwater harvesting, this could greatly improve urban water problems in the future.

Evidence

THE FUTURE

This graph shows two predictions for the amount of water in cubic kilometers the world's people will be using per year by 2025. The red line is the amount of water that will be used if current rates of use continue as usual. The blue line, or preferable rate, shows the amount that will be used if people use water more productively and sustainably.

What will you do to help ensure a preferable future for water supplies?

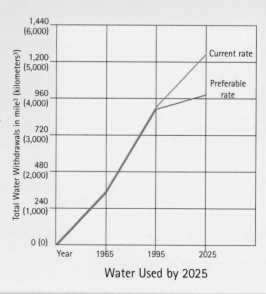

Water Used by 2025

Global Citizenship

Global citizenship is when individuals recognize that they are citizens of the world and that their actions can have an impact on the rest of the planet. When people accept this interdependency, they also accept their responsibility to make changes. Everyone can make small changes and use less water in their everyday lives. People can also think more carefully about the things they buy and the waste that they produce.

▶ In 2005, the UN launched "The Decade of Water." Leaders of countries in the UN all pledged to try and halve the number of people in the world without an improved water supply by 2015. Positive actions like these by world leaders are an important step in the right direction.

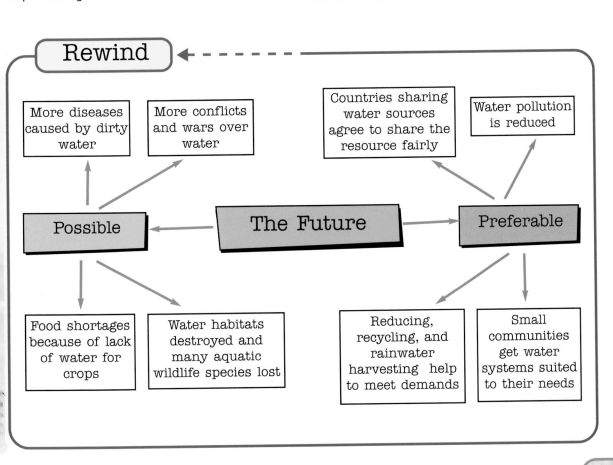

Glossary, Further Information, and Web Sites

Aquifer An area of rock that is porous and is saturated with water.

Eutrophication The process by which a body of water is enriched with nutrients, causing it to fill with aquatic plants and algae that may deplete the oxygen supply in the water.

Dengue An infectious disease spread by mosquitoes that causes a rash, severe joint pain, and headaches.

Fresh water Water that is not salty and is safe for people to use.

Hydroelectric power A method of generating electricity by converting the energy of running water into electric power.

Hydroponics A method of growing plants in water containing dissolved nutrients instead of in soil.

Infiltration The process by which rainwater seeps or filters through rocks and soil under the ground.

Interdependent Describes organisms and habitats that need each other for survival.

Irrigation To supply water by artificial means, particularly to fields, to improve crop growth and yields.

Malaria An infectious disease spread by mosquitoes that causes periods of chills, fever, and sweating.

Natural resource A material that is part of the natural world, such as water, soil, air, trees, and fossil fuels, which people use or rely on.

Photosynthesis The process by which plants use energy and carbon dioxide to produce their own food.

River basin The area of land from which rainwater or streams drain into a river.

Runoff The fertilizers, pesticides, and other pollutants that can be washed off the land by rain and can flow into rivers and other water supplies.

Sustainable Carried out without depleting or permanently damaging resources. Sustainable forestry is when people replant trees and manage woodland when they harvest timber and other products.

Vendor A person who sells something.

Water table The level below which soil and rock are saturated with water.

Books to read

Disasters Up Close: Droughts
Michael Woods (Lerner Publications, 2006)

Green Alert: Polluted Waters
Jennifer Stefanow (Raintree, 2004)

Nature's Cycles: The Water Cycle
Sally Morgan (Powerkids Press, 2009)

The Pros and Cons of Water Power
Richard and Louise Spilsbury (Rosen, 2007)

Turbulent Planet, Wild Water: Floods
Tony Allan (Raintree, 2005)

Web Sites

Due to the changing nature of Internet links, Rosen Publishing has developed an online list of Web sites related to the subject of this book. This site is regularly updated. Please use this link to access this list: www.rosenlinks.com/ces/wate

Topic Web

Use this topic web to discover themes and ideas in subjects that are related to water supply.

English and Literacy

- Eyewitness accounts of flood disasters and living in regions during times of severe drought.
- Debate the pros and cons of making water a human right or keeping it as a commodity to be bought and sold for profit.
- Read accounts of the lives of people who have been displaced by dams and forced to rebuild their lives somewhere new.

History and Economics

- Development along the length of major rivers.
- How people use water resources for fishing, recreation and tourism, irrigation, and energy production.

Geography

- Consider the impacts of flood disasters and how people deal with them.
- Study a section of a river and its valley and the changes that take place downstream (caused by weathering and erosion) plus the global patterns created by major river systems, including deltas.

Science and the Environment

- Environmental problems such as pollution, including ocean pollution.
- The effects of human activity on the ecology of aquatic habitats.
- Test evaporation of salt water and other dissolved water solutions and other methods of purifying water, such as sieving and filtering.

Water Supply

Art and Culture

- Take photographs of water and water habitats from different viewpoints, recording aspects of the natural environment and made features.
- Music and culture of different people who live alongside one of the world's major rivers, such as the Ganges or Nile.

Index